A Pod of Dolphins

and Other Sea Mammal Groups

Richard Spilsbury

Heinemann
LIBRARY
Chicago, Illinois

www.capstonepub.com
Visit our website to find out more information about Heinemann-Raintree books.

To order:

☎ Phone 800-747-4992

🖥 Visit www.capstonepub.com to browse our catalog and order online.

© 2013 Heinemann Library
an imprint of Capstone Global Library, LLC
Chicago, Illinois

Edited by Nancy Dickmann, Adam Miller, and Laura Knowles
Designed by Richard Parker
Picture research by Ruth Blair
Original Illustrations © Capstone Global Library Ltd 2013
Illustrations by Jeff Edwards

Originated by Capstone Global Library Ltd
Printed and bound in China by CTPS

16 15 14 13 12
10 9 8 7 6 5 4 3 2 1

Library of Congress Cataloging-in-Publication Data
Spilsbury, Richard, 1963-
  A pod of dolphins, and other sea mammal groups / Richard Spilsbury.
      p. cm.—(Animals in groups)
  Includes bibliographical references and index.
  ISBN 978-1-4329-6483-2 (hb)—ISBN 978-1-4329-6490-0 (pb) 1. Dolphins—Juvenile literature. 2. Marine mammals—Juvenile literature. I. Title.
  QL737.C432S577 2013
  599.53—dc23   2011038140

Acknowledgments
We would like to thank the following for permission to reproduce photographs: Corbis pp. 11 (© HO/Reuters), 14 (© Ocean), 17 (© Anthony Pierce/Specialist Stock), 31 (© Albert Gea/Reuters), 32 (© Stuart Westmorland), 38 (© Sanford/Agliolo); Dreamstime.com p. 8 (© Wiltding); iStockphoto p. 5 (© David Schrader); Naturepl pp. 10 (© Wild Wonders of Europe/Campbell), 13 (© Mark Carwardine), 19 (© TOM WALMSLEY), 24 (© Todd Pusser), 25 (© Doug Perrine), 27 (© Jurgen Freund), 30 (© Nature Production), 35 (© David Fleetham), 39 (© LYNN M. STONE), 41 (© Aflo); Science Photo Library p. 15 (LAWRENCE MIGDALE); Shutterstock pp. 4 (© Hiroshi Sato), 7 (© Willyam Bradberry), 16 (© pmld), 18 (© Elena Larina), 21, 29 (© Four Oaks), 22 (© guentermanaus), 33 (© joyfuldesigns), 37 (© Achim Baque).

Cover photograph of bottlenose dolphins (Tursiops truncatus) in the Caribbean Sea near Roatan, Honduras, reproduced with permission of Corbis (© Stuart Westmorland/Science Faction).

Every effort has been made to contact copyright holders of any material reproduced in this book. Any omissions will be rectified in subsequent printings if notice is given to the publisher.

Disclaimer
All the Internet addresses (URLs) given in this book were valid at the time of going to press. However, due to the dynamic nature of the Internet, some addresses may have changed, or sites may have changed or ceased to exist since publication. While the author and publisher regret any inconvenience this may cause readers, no responsibility for any such changes can be accepted by either the author or the publisher.

Contents

DID YOU KNOW?

Discover amazing facts about dolphins.

HUMAN INTERACTION

Find out what happens when humans and dolphins come into contact with each other.

Some words are shown in bold, **like this.** You can find out what they mean by looking in the glossary.

HABITAT IN DANGER

Learn how dolphins' habitats are under threat, and what is being done to protect them.

Welcome to the Pod!

Dolphins are curious, intelligent **mammals** that are **adapted** for spending their entire lives in water. Like other mammals, dolphins need to breathe air. They rise to the surface, open the **blowhole** on top of their head to breathe, and then close the blowhole when they dive again.

Dolphins and whales

There are 39 types, or **species**, of dolphins living worldwide. Most, including the well-known bottlenose dolphin, live in the shallower parts of oceans. A few types live only in rivers, such as the Amazon River in Brazil.

blowhole

beak

dorsal fin

flipper

tail

Dolphins have a sleek, pointed shape with a strong tail to swim fast. They use their flippers and dorsal fin to steer through the water.

Dolphins, like sperm whales, are toothed whales. This means they have pointed teeth for catching **prey**. Most of the largest whales in the world, including the blue whale, are **baleen** whales. Their mouths have rows of tough, comb-like structures (called baleen) to filter animals to eat from the water.

Group living

Dolphins spend some time alone—for example, when sleeping—but they usually swim together in groups. These groups are called pods or schools.

This pod of dolphins is moving together through the ocean.

DID YOU KNOW?

Dolphins sleep around eight hours each day, in several bursts of about two hours each. They can rest at the surface, on the shallow seabed, or even while swimming. Only half their brain sleeps at a time, so they can keep a lookout for **predators** and return to the surface regularly to breathe!

What Are Dolphin Pods Like?

There is no single type of dolphin pod. Some pods can have just a few individuals, but others may contain many thousands of dolphins!

Why live in groups?

Animals live in groups for two main reasons. The first is that they can help one another find the things they need, such as food or other individuals to **breed** with. The second is that group members can look out for danger from predators and warn others.

The largest dolphin pods form when they travel across open, deep water. Small pods may even group together into bigger ones, sometimes called superpods, in these conditions. This is because the waters may be less well known and there is more risk of danger. There is greater safety in numbers.

Where pods go

Some dolphin pods always stay in the same areas, where they know they can find enough food as well as clean or undisturbed waters that will not harm them. These areas are called **home ranges**. Home ranges are bigger when there is less prey available, because dolphins then need to cover greater distances to get the food they need.

Other pods **migrate** between different areas of ocean. For example, some bottlenose dolphins live and feed in northern parts of the Atlantic Ocean in the summer, and they then swim to warmer waters near the equator in the winter. The equator is an imaginary circle around Earth where the temperatures remain warm all year round.

An average pod contains around 10 dolphins, but this varies by species. For example, bottlenose dolphin pods (shown here) usually have between three and fifteen members, while spinner dolphin pods often have hundreds of members.

Different pods

There are different types of dolphin pods made up of different sorts of individuals. For instance, **bachelor pods** contain just bulls (males). Other pods may contain just young dolphins of both sexes.

Nursery pods contain several dolphin cows (females) with their most recent calves (babies).

Pod leaders

Pods usually have leaders that make decisions about where the group goes and what it does. The leaders of animal groups are often called **dominant** individuals. Dominant dolphins are usually bigger and older than the rest. In general, this means they can fight better against other dolphins and against predators. It means they are more experienced at **navigating** underwater to find food or safe waters to live in. So, a bigger, older cow (female) will often be dominant over a smaller one.

In general, bulls are dominant over cows, because they usually grow to a larger size. Dominant bulls may breed with several cows in a pod, whereas less important, or **subordinate**, bulls do not. It is not always easy to tell which dolphin is dominant, but one way is to look for the dolphin that swims nearer to the front or surface in the pod.

HUMAN INTERACTION

In some countries, such as Japan, people hunt dolphins to eat or to sell to aquariums around the world. They chase pods with fast boats and bang on metal rods underwater. This scares and confuses the dolphins. Dominant dolphins lead the pods toward land, in an attempt to reach safer, shallower waters. However, people lie in wait with nets and weapons to trap and slaughter the dolphins in bays.

Moving around

Pods often swim in particular formations, or patterns. For example, a navigating formation is a wedge-shaped group. It is led by the dominant dolphin at the front point, with cows and calves behind. Parade formations look like a circle, square, or line of dolphins from above. Dolphins swimming in a parade pod sometimes leap out of the water. This is called porpoising. It reduces the drag, or pull, of water on the skin of the dolphins that can slow them down.

HUMAN INTERACTION

Many dolphin pods take it easy when swimming by bowriding. This is when they are pushed along by the wave formed by the bow (front) of a moving ship.

Bowriding dolphins get the best push within a few feet of the front of a moving boat or ship.

Out of water

Sometimes pods swim into shallow water or even onto beaches. This is called **stranding**. Stranding may be accidental if the dominant dolphin makes a mistake in navigation. But it may be on purpose when pod members become sick, wounded, or distressed. In shallow water, dolphins need less effort to stay near the surface and breathe. Some stranded dolphins swim back to sea, but others may die.

A woman keeps a stranded dolphin's skin cool in the Sun until it can be helped back into the sea.

DID YOU KNOW?

Pacific spotted dolphins can swim at up to 25 miles (40 kilometers) per hour for short bursts. This is over four times the speed of the fastest human swimmer. However, dolphins usually cruise along at around a quarter of their top speed.

How Do Dolphin Pods Communicate?

Animals in groups need to communicate to stay together, to share information about dangers and places to feed, and to recognize different group members. Dolphins communicate with each other in many different ways. One of the most important ways is by using sound. One reason for this is that dolphins often swim at night or in deep, dark water, where seeing each other is almost impossible.

Dolphin sounds

Dolphins make around 30 different sounds, including squeaks, grunts, screams, and "raspberries"! But dolphins make most sounds underwater by forcing air through tubes inside their noses. A lump of special fat in their forehead called a **melon** directs the sound into the water. Sounds travel as ripples underwater.

Dolphin hearing

Dolphins only have tiny ear holes the width of pinholes, and they have no earlobes. They "hear" sounds by feeling ripples against the skin on their jaws or even their teeth. The **vibrations** travel through their jaws to their ears. The dolphin's brain recognizes the vibration patterns as different sounds.

HABITAT IN DANGER

Noises made by boats and ships are affecting how well dolphins communicate using sound. These noises include the rumble of engines and sonar. Sonar is when sound is used to figure out water depth and seafloor shape. Some scientists believe that sonar confuses dolphins, so they are more likely to become stranded.

Dolphins create some sounds at the surface by blowing air through their blowhole and changing its shape. Think of how you make noises when releasing air from a balloon!

Individual whistle

We can usually recognize each other by the sound of our voices. Dolphins recognize each other by their **signature whistle**. This is a whistle unique to each dolphin. Dolphins may learn another dolphin's whistle and copy it to make contact with a particular individual in their pod. They may alter their signature whistle to tell other dolphins how they are feeling. For example, they whistle louder when distressed and faster when the pod is about to hunt.

Dolphins clap their teeth together loudly when fighting, to tell others to back off. They also make this sound during play, to say who is winning.

DID YOU KNOW?

Dolphin brains are about the same size as human brains. However, the part of the brain that processes sounds is up to 40 times bigger than that in humans.

Sound meanings

The other main types of dolphin sounds are repeated in sequences. These may be either continuous "trains" or regular bursts (pulses) of sounds, including clicks and squeaks. Dolphins produce a buzzing "**click-train**" when they are approaching something of interest in the water. Sometimes there are as many as 2,000 clicks per second! They produce squeak pulses when trapped.

Scientists record and study sounds of different dolphin species and watch their behavior to figure out what different sounds might mean.

Body language

Winking, waving, smiling, or shrugging our shoulders are all ways we pass on messages to each other without using words. Dolphins also communicate using different types of body language, although scientists are not sure what some of the gestures, or movements, mean. Some communicate annoyance or anger with repeated sharp head jerks, known as snitting. A dolphin that rolls upside down or "plays dead" next to another dolphin is showing that it is subordinate.

A dolphin that is feeling annoyed will often smack its tail on the water.

HUMAN INTERACTION

Scientists in Hawaii taught captive dolphins to understand sign language using gestures that represented words and actions. For example, when dolphins were shown gestures meaning "Right Basket Frisbee Left In," they put the Frisbee on their left into the basket on their right!

Spinner dolphins are the most acrobatic dolphins.

Acrobatics

Dolphins sometimes leap high from the water, even spinning or somersaulting before they splash back into the water. This is called **breaching**, and it is sometimes used for communicating. Spinner dolphins get their name from their characteristic leaps and barrel-roll spins. These happen most often when they are in a big, moving pod. Scientists think dolphins spin and splash to make it obvious to others in their pod where they are and the direction they are swimming.

DID YOU KNOW?

Spinner dolphins can complete as many as 14 jumps in a row, and they may perform 7 barrel-rolls in each jump!

Touch

Dolphins also communicate through physical contact. Their skin, especially on their beaks and fins, is very sensitive to touch. Pod members may nuzzle, rest their fin on another's back or fin, or rub against each other to strengthen bonds.

Dolphins make close contact to form and strengthen friendships among pod members.

Pod fights

Fights sometimes happen in dolphin pods over which dolphin is dominant over others. Dolphins are like most other animals: they avoid fighting when possible because of the risk of injury. They communicate to other dolphins that they are ready to fight, but they hope that this message is enough to decide the argument. For instance, they may hump their back and raise their head so their body forms an S-shape, like that of an aggressive shark. When threats do not work, dolphins may fight—for example, by swimming fast and ramming each other using their hard beaks.

Dolphins sometimes fight by raking their sharp teeth on the sensitive skin of others. This may be where the scar above this animal's eye came from.

Predators

The only natural threats to dolphins are from large sharks and orcas. Dolphins usually try to swim faster than these powerful predators, rather than fight. However, pods of dolphins sometimes work together to attack smaller sharks by butting their soft undersides or **gills**.

DID YOU KNOW?

Fighting dolphins may tail-whip, or move their tail fast through the water toward their opponents. This produces a moving wall of water that may knock the other dolphin off balance.

How Do Dolphin Groups Feed?

One of the major benefits of living in a pod is finding and hunting food together. This saves time and effort compared to hunting alone. Dolphins eat mostly fish. The types of fish vary according to where they live. Dolphins living in oceans often hunt fish living in big **shoals**, such as sardines, mackerels, and anchovies. They also catch squid. River dolphins eat fish such as carp and catfish, but also shrimp and crabs.

Dolphins usually eat around one-twentieth of their body weight each day. For an adult, that is around 22 to 44 pounds (10 to 20 kilograms). The largest single fish a dolphin would eat is about 11 pounds (5 kilograms).

Fish eaters

Dolphins have rows of sharp, cone-shaped teeth that help them grip the smooth scales and slimy skin of fish. Spinner dolphins have over 250 identical teeth, which is more than any other mammal. Amazon river dolphins have some flattened teeth at the back of their jaws. They use them to crush the hard bodies of catfish before swallowing. Dolphins usually swallow their prey whole.

HABITAT IN DANGER

People are catching so many wild fish that populations are falling around the world. This means there is more competition between fishermen and dolphins over the remaining fish. Some fishermen kill dolphins because they claim the dolphins are taking the fish they need to catch to make a living.

Dolphins have just one set of teeth to last their whole lives. If they get broken, no teeth will grow to replace them.

Hunting using sound

Most dolphins can spot prey, but they cannot rely on sight alone for hunting. This is because they often hunt in deep, dark ocean water or cloudy rivers. Instead, dolphins use sound for hunting in a process called **echolocation**. They produce click-trains that are focused in a beam by their melon. The noise sounds similar to a constantly creaking door or a buzzing insect.

The Amazon river dolphin's eyes are tiny, since sight is not a very useful sense for finding a meal in the muddy waters there.

DID YOU KNOW?

Ganges and Indus river dolphins are almost blind, but they have especially large melons in their heads. This is because they rely totally on echolocation for getting around and finding food in the murky rivers.

When the sound ripples strike an object, such as a fish or buried crab, some bounce back. The dolphin hears the echo, and its brain compares this with the original click-train. Using echolocation, dolphins can detect objects up to around 330 feet (100 meters) away and as narrow as a toothbrush bristle. All members of a dolphin pod can echolocate in the same waters without colliding, because each can recognize its own click-trains.

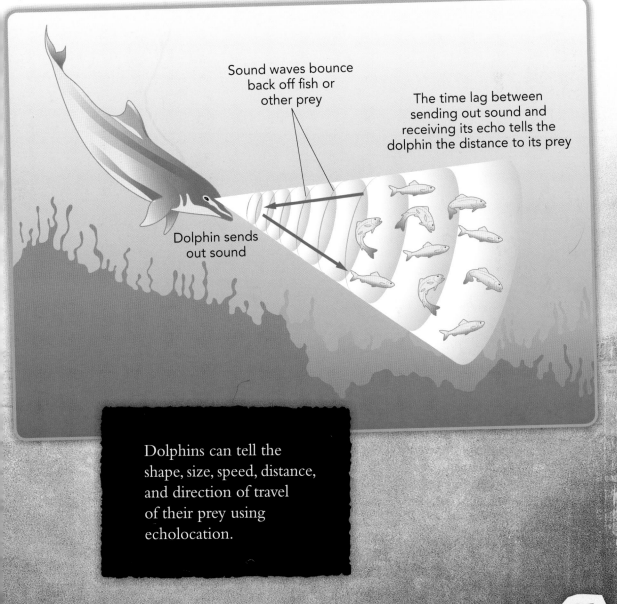

Sound waves bounce back off fish or other prey

The time lag between sending out sound and receiving its echo tells the dolphin the distance to its prey

Dolphin sends out sound

Dolphins can tell the shape, size, speed, distance, and direction of travel of their prey using echolocation.

Pod meals

Once they have located prey, dolphins often catch food together with other pod members, usually in small groups. They use several amazing techniques to do this.

- *Corralling*: Pod members swim toward a shoal of fish from different sides, forming a tight circle around it. They take turns swimming fast into the corralled fish to feed, while the others prevent fish from escaping.

- *Herding*: Pods sometimes herd shoals of fish onto sloping mud banks or sand bars. The fish cannot easily escape from the shallow water, and the dolphins glide ashore to take a mouthful before sliding back into the water.

- *Mud netting*: Some bottlenose dolphins in Australia swim in circles in shallow water, wagging their tails in the mud. This both disturbs fish in the mud and creates a ring of muddy water that traps them. The fish panic and leap out of the circle, where dolphins wait with their mouths open.

- *Spitting*: Snubfin dolphins sometimes raise their heads and spit water on the surface. This brings fish to the surface, and the dolphins eat them.

Herding onto beaches is sometimes called strand-feeding.

HUMAN INTERACTION

Dolphins sometimes work with fishermen to increase one another's catch! For example, the Irrawaddy dolphin in eastern India and Southeast Asia herds shoals of fish toward waiting nets. Fishermen catch up to three times more fish this way, and the dolphins feed on cornered fish and those that fall from nets. Unfortunately, the dolphins often get caught up in the nets, too. This has led to the Irrawaddy dolphin becoming **endangered**.

Mixed pods

Some pods are made up of different species of dolphins. The group moves together, and the different species rely on one another for safety in greater numbers. However, they do not compete over the same food. For example, spotted and spinner dolphins form large pods in warmer parts of the Atlantic Ocean. The spotted dolphins feed on prey near the surface, such as herring. Spinner dolphins feed farther down, often at night, on squid and small fish.

Dolphins are an important part of the ocean food web. The Sun provides energy to plant life. Arrows point from each living thing to an animal that eats it.

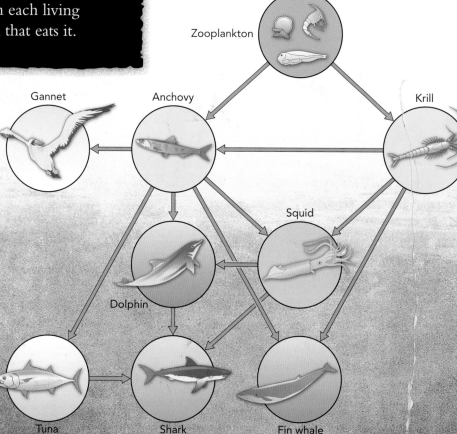

SUN

Phytoplankton

Zooplankton

Gannet

Anchovy

Krill

Squid

Dolphin

Tuna

Shark

Fin whale

Feeding associations

Dolphins share their ocean **habitats** with many other fish-eating animals. These include large fish such as tuna and sharks and seabirds such as gannets and gulls. They also include mammals such as sea lions, minke whales, and humpback whales. Dolphins are especially good at locating shoals of fish and corralling them near the surface, so seabirds often follow pods to take advantage of their finds. Shoals of big yellowfin tuna also follow below pods of spinner and other dolphins at the surface, because they help them locate shoals of smaller prey.

This fisherman is pulling a line-caught, dolphin-friendly tuna onto his boat.

HUMAN INTERACTION

People have followed dolphins to locate tuna for centuries. In the recent past, millions of dolphins were trapped, crushed, and drowned in the enormous nets used to catch the valuable tuna. Today, this cruelty to dolphins is avoided, mostly because people catch tuna on long lines with hooks from fishing boats instead.

How Do Dolphins Care for Young?

Dolphins usually breed in the warmer months of the year. Cows are around eight years old when they can first breed, but bulls are much older. This is because they only get the chance to breed if they are dominant members in a pod. Bulls in bachelor pods show off their strength and fitness to cows in the breeding season by breaching and threatening or fighting other males.

Birth

Pregnant cows give birth to a single calf around 8 to 16 months after mating. There is often another cow swimming close to the mother, acting like a **midwife**. The calf is born tail-first, to reduce the risk of drowning. It might breathe in water if it were born head-first. The midwife may help with delivery by tugging the tail or whistling with encouragement.

The mother or midwife then gently lifts the newborn calf to the surface so it can take its first few breaths. This is because newborns tend to sink, since they have no air in their lungs to help them float. The midwife keeps an eye on the calf for several weeks after birth, especially if its mother is off hunting.

HABITAT IN DANGER

Water pollution caused by people harms dolphins, particularly calves. In the Mekong River between 2003 and 2009, nearly two-thirds of all dead river dolphins were under two weeks old. Farming chemicals in the water had weakened their ability to survive infections that healthy dolphins could easily recover from.

To impress cows during breeding season, bull dolphins sometimes move backward on their tails.

Baby dolphins

Newborn calves measure around 24 to 47 inches (60 to 120 centimeters) long. They are usually darker in color than adults, and they sometimes have light stripes from being folded up inside their mother. Calves feed on milk from their mothers, like other mammals. Dolphin milk is full of fat and allows calves to grow thick layers of **blubber** under their skin. This is important to maintain the right body temperature, even when dolphins swim through areas of water with different temperatures.

A cow squirts milk from folds in the skin on her underside when the calf nuzzles her.

A calf stays by its mother's side for several years, learning how to survive.

The early years

Cows generally care for their calves for three to six years. Some calves feed on milk for 18 months, yet most start to eat some fish from around 6 months. At first, cows catch fish for their calves. They may break them up into pieces to make them easier to eat by slapping them on the water surface or seabed. In the first six months, calves develop their signature whistle, which is often similar to their mother's.

DID YOU KNOW?

Neither calves nor their mothers sleep for the first few months after birth. This is to make sure the calves do not drown while sleeping, and also to look out for any predators that might easily catch a weak calf.

Learning

Dolphins are very clever and learn skills quickly. Calves learn a lot from their mother. They watch and hear her echolocating, hunting, and interacting with other pod members in different ways. When calves get too aggressive, cows may discipline them by lifting them out of the water using their flippers. This is a useful lesson to learn for fitting into the pod.

Dolphins sometimes learn very unique skills. For example, a group of female bottlenose dolphins in Australia uses sponges as tools to help them catch fish. The sponge protects their beak as they scatter sand from the rocky seabed to find hiding fish. Cows teach calves, especially females, to find and use sponges in this special way.

This dolphin is investigating a piece of seaweed and how it sinks in the water.

Play

Dolphins of all ages like to play. For example, they may play with feathers, stones, seaweed, and unfamiliar objects they find in the water. They may surf on waves and use their fins to create whirlpools in the water to blow bubble rings into. For young dolphins, play is especially important to improve their skills. For example, playing chase with other dolphins develops echolocation skills and speed through the water, both of which are very important for successful hunting.

Many people believe keeping dolphins in small tanks and away from pod members is cruel.

HUMAN INTERACTION

Dolphins are very good at learning tricks. This is the main reason why some people capture wild dolphins to keep in **dolphinariums** and aquariums to entertain the public.

What Are Other Sea Mammal Groups Like?

Many other types of mammals live in the oceans. They are adapted for life in the water, and some of them live in groups like dolphins.

Humpback whales

Humpback whales are baleen whales that live throughout the oceans, including the coldest waters near the poles. They grow up to around 50 feet (15 meters) long, with flippers that are around one-third the length of their bodies.

Female humpbacks usually live in small family groups of a cow and her calf. Bulls may live alone or in bachelor pods. Humpbacks may form larger, mixed-sex, temporary groups each year in warm, tropical waters where they meet to breed. Humpbacks travel long distances between breeding and feeding grounds near the poles. They also form temporary groups when they feed together in summer feeding grounds.

Humpbacks feed on shoals of small, shrimp-like animals called krill or on fish such as anchovies. The group sometimes feeds together by bubble-netting. This is when they blow rings of bubbles around shoals to force them together and up near the surface. The whales then swim up underneath and take an enormous mouthful. They strain the water out from their mouths through their baleen and swallow the captured prey.

DID YOU KNOW?

Male humpback whales sing during the breeding season. Their songs are complicated sequences of rumbles, grunts, and whistles that can last up to half an hour and that they repeat for hours.

Humpback whales such as this one spend most of their time in small, family groups.

Walruses

Walruses are enormous relatives of seals, with long, pointed teeth, called tusks, and long whiskers. Unlike whales, these sea mammals spend some time out of water on floating sea ice or rocky shores. They feed on the muddy seabed under cold, shallow Arctic waters. Walruses, like whales, have thick blubber to stay warm in the cold. They dive and use their sensitive whiskers to find clams and mussels. Then they blow jets of water or wave their flippers to clear the mud from their food.

For most of the year, bull walruses live in small bachelor **herds**, while cows and calves live in separate nursery herds. During the spring breeding season, they come together, forming enormous herds of up to 5,000 individuals. The bulls display their tusks, bellow, charge, and fight each other to show dominance. The largest bulls with the longest tusks are usually dominant. Their prize is being able to breed with several cows.

Cows give birth on ice floes, and the calves remain on the ice, out of the reach of predators such as orcas, for their first two years. Cows in the nursery herd take turns watching over calves while their mothers are at sea feeding.

HABITAT IN DANGER

Walruses are under threat from **climate change**. One reason is that Arctic seas are getting warmer, so there is less sea ice. Cows must leave their young for longer and need to swim farther to reach areas of seabed that are rich in food.

Walruses rest, sleep, fight, and breed on land while they wait for the ice to form.

Sea otters

Sea otters are the heaviest members of the weasel family, and they live in coastal waters of the northern Pacific Ocean. They dive up to 328 feet (100 meters) to hunt sea urchins, crabs, and sea snails to eat. Sea otters usually eat at the surface while floating on their backs. They sometimes rest a flat stone on their belly, grip a shell, and bash it against the stone to open it.

Groups of sea otters are called rafts. In a raft, some floating otters doze, while others watch for predators such as orcas and sea lions. The otters stop rolling waves from carrying them away from the raft by holding paws or by wrapping themselves in strong seaweed growing from the seabed. Rafts usually contain around 15 to 20 otters, but sometimes there are hundreds.

Rafts are always made up of either just females, with any young pups, or just males.

Sea otters eat up to a quarter of their weight in food each day. For large males, that is as much as 25 pounds (11 kilograms)!

Female rafts often form in home ranges patrolled by males. These contain food and sheltered waters where otters can rest. Males breed with the females in their home range. They often keep other males away from this area by splashing water rather than by fighting.

HABITAT IN DANGER

Sea otters have the densest fur of any animal. It traps warm air so that they do not get too cold in the water. When oil tankers and wells spill oil into the sea, it affects sea otters badly. This is because they cannot clean the sticky oil from their fur and end up dying from the cold.

How Can We Protect Dolphins?

Being in a pod is important to dolphins, just like being in a family or group of friends or class is to you. Dolphins in a pod share many activities together. They hunt, feed, swim, and raise young. Communication is very important for keeping the group together and doing the same things. Being in a group provides opportunities to breed and safety in numbers against predators. Nevertheless, group living can also cause problems. For example, pods of dolphins follow fish that people want to catch. Hundreds of thousands of dolphins die in the nets of the world's fishing ships each year.

Meeting dolphins

In some places, people pay to swim with dolphins. However, the dolphins are sometimes brought in from other countries, far from their own pods, and are trapped close to the shore using nets. They may share the water with many people. Some people have been injured by dolphins, and dolphins are at risk of catching illnesses from people. Around 13 million people go whale watching from boats each year. The best tours keep a safe distance from the animals so that they are not frightened or at risk from propellers.

HUMAN INTERACTION

The word SMART is a way to remember how to watch wild dolphins from boats without harming them:

Stay at least 165 feet (50 meters) away.
Move away slowly if the dolphins show signs of disturbance.
Always stop the engine.
Refrain from swimming with, touching, or feeding wild dolphins.
Teach others to follow these rules.

Dolphins are fascinating to watch, but we must be careful not to harm them.

Fact File

DOLPHIN COLOR

Most dolphins are gray in color, but some are pink or almost white. Some dolphins have patterned skin. For example, hourglass dolphins are black and white, common dolphins have stripes of gray and yellow, and adult spotted dolphins have light spots all over.

DOLPHIN SIZE

The largest member of the dolphin family is the orca. Males can weigh up to 10 tons and measure nearly 33 feet (10 meters) in length. In comparison, humpback whales are twice as long and four times as heavy! The smallest dolphin species is Maui's dolphin, which measures 4 feet (1.2 meters), or about the same length as a sea otter.

DOLPHIN LIFESPAN

The average lifespan of a dolphin in the wild is about 30 years, but in **captivity**, dolphins have lived to 45 years. However, half of all captured dolphins die within their first two years of captivity. Reasons include illnesses resulting from stress caused by being separated from their pod or from being kept in cold or **chlorinated water**.

DOLPHIN DIVING

Bottlenose dolphins can dive nearly 2,000 feet (more than 600 meters) deep to locate food, but they usually dive much shallower distances. The U.S. Navy keeps and trains dolphins to dive and detect enemy sea mines and to retrieve equipment dropped by naval ships and airplanes!

ENDANGERED OR COMMON?

The most endangered dolphin is the Yangtze river dolphin, which has been sighted so rarely it is now thought to have died out, and Maui's dolphin, with around 100 animals. The common dolphin lives up to its name, with a global population of around 3 million—five times more than bottlenose dolphins.

This map shows which areas of the world's oceans dolphins live in.

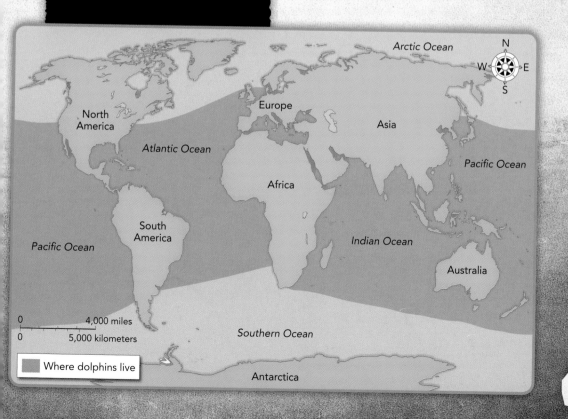

Arctic Ocean

North America

Europe

Asia

Atlantic Ocean

Africa

Pacific Ocean

South America

Indian Ocean

Pacific Ocean

Australia

| 0 | 4,000 miles |
| 0 | 5,000 kilometers |

Southern Ocean

Where dolphins live

Antarctica

Glossary

adapted having physical features or ways of behaving that help an animal survive in a particular habitat

bachelor pod group of male dolphins or other whales

baleen tough, comb-like structure in a whale's mouth used to filter food from the water

blowhole hole in the top of a whale's head that it uses to breathe through

blubber thick, fatty layer underneath the skin of sea mammals that helps them stay warm in cold water

breaching leaping clear of the water

breed when living things get together to produce young

captivity being kept in an enclosed zoo or park, instead of living in the wild

chlorinated water water that has had a substance called chlorine added to it, such as swimming pool water

click-train type of call made up of a sequence of clicks, produced by dolphins or other whales

climate change changes in the world's weather patterns caused by human activity

dolphinarium building with a pool where people can go to see dolphins, especially those trained to do tricks

dominant more important or powerful

echolocation use of echoes to find things

endangered at risk of dying out

gills parts of the body used by fish and other animals to breathe underwater

habitat natural home or surroundings of a living thing

herd group of animals of the same type that live and feed together

home range area of land or sea where an animal lives and finds food

mammal animal that feeds its young on milk from the mother's body

melon fatty organ in a dolphin's forehead

midwife person who helps a woman give birth to a baby

migrate move from one part of the world to another, often in order to feed or breed in better conditions

navigate find the route or direction across an area to reach a chosen destination

predator animal that hunts and eats other animals

prey animal that is hunted and eaten by another animal

shoal large group of fish swimming together

signature whistle type of individual whistling call made by a dolphin

species particular type of living thing

stranding when dolphins or whales swim onto shores and become stuck

subordinate less important member of a group

vibration shaking

Find Out More

Books

Davidson, Susanna. *Whales and Dolphins* (Usborne Discovery). Tulsa, Okla.: EDC, 2008.

Hoyt, Erich. *Whale Rescue: Changing the Future for Endangered Wildlife* (Firefly Animal Rescue). Buffalo, N.Y.: Firefly, 2005.

Llewellyn, Claire. *Oceans* (Habitat Survival). Chicago: Raintree, 2013.

Parker, Steve. *Whales and Dolphins* (100 Things You Should Know About). Broomall, Pa.: Mason Crest, 2011.

Web sites

www.bluevoice.org

Blue Voice is a group dedicated to protecting dolphins, whales, and the natural environments that they live in. Visit its web site to find more details about the group's work, facts about dolphins, and how you can help save dolphins and whales.

kids.nationalgeographic.com/kids/animals/creaturefeature

You can find out lots of interesting and exciting information about your favorite dolphins and whales at the National Geographic web site. Click on "bottlenose dolphins" and other animals of interest on this page.

Places to visit

Many natural history museums have excellent collections of dolphin and whale skeletons and information. You could visit the National Museum of Natural History in Washington, D.C., or find out if there is a natural history museum near you.

Would you like to see dolphins or whales in the wild? Perhaps you might be lucky enough to go on a whale-watching boat trip. There are also some areas of coast where it is possible to spot whales from the shore. These experiences are possible on the east and west coasts of the United States, and along the Gulf of Mexico in the southern part of the country.

More topics to research

This book only tells you some of the things that might interest you about dolphins and other sea mammals. Go to the library to find out more. For example, how do they hold their breath for long, deep dives? In what ways are whales different from fish? Whales have many adaptations to life in oceans, but how are other mammals adapted to their habitats and lifestyles? Here are three interesting mammals to research that have amazing adaptations for living in their different habitats: camels in deserts, bats active by night, and mole-rats underground.

Index